Sweet Poison

Poetry

Shaolin Poe

POEMS

To My Father
Thank you for always encouraging my love of poetry.

PREFACE

Some of these poems are stories. Some are my deepest, private feelings. Some are my efforts to understand how other people see the world.

I leave it to you to decide which is which, though I'd prefer that something in this collection resonate with you and tell your story in new words, becoming yours.

PARADIGM SHIFT

Has it changed?
Or is it not
Exactly as it was before?

Has the world
Turned upside down
And inside-out from core?

My world is shattered
Torn apart
The feast of ravening beasts.

My hope snuffed out
My pathway lost
My heart a drought of peace.

But yet I cannot
In my frantic,
Frightened, frenzy find

What has changed.
For nothing
Has been altered but my mind.

What folly
What hypocrisy
We embrace with lies

As if our blind
Complacency
And charitable guise

Paired with feigned
Sincerity
And half averted eyes

Will prove to hold
The least excuse
For our reluctant lives

Or offer any
Consolation
For embittered cries

That we will weep
When we are forced
To recognize our prize.

Has it changed?
Or is it not
Exactly as it was before?

I cannot tell
For I am lost
And all that I adore

Is lost to me
And though I feel
A void in place of love

I cannot help
But pray my tears
Are heard from up above.

For I am lost
And all I thought I had
Is lost to me

And I am at a loss
Of who I am
And how to be.

I have no mentor
I may ask
And the guidance given me

Is missing
Pertinent parts
Perhaps precluding what I see.

I hurt
I ache
I grope in dark

I pray
I will not
Miss the mark

For though I think
I see things
Exactly as they are

SHAOLIN POE

I see through a glass
But darkly
And the end is very far.

Has it changed?
Or is it not
Exactly as it was before?

For nothing
Has been altered
Just my eyes have opened more.

FRAGMENTATION

A house divided against itself,
Never shall it stand
"It's truth," proclaimed the luminary
A smart, sagacious man.

My walls are fast collapsing then,
As only I can see,
For my life is one of separation--
Division within me.

WHERE IS HERE?

Among the thorns and stormy skies
Beyond the lands and friends I know
Amidst the laughter and the cries
From Heav'n above to Hell below

My mind it flutters listlessly
Flickering on the bounds of thought
Thrown at me most endlessly
The hopes of what my heart has sought.

The swirling smoke of hopes and dreams
That twist and curl as my hungers change,
The fantasy that baits my view
And with a puff is rearranged—

What can I see of what is here?
For what is here to me—
Within the smoke of others' views
May be far from reality.

ABSENCE

Absence makes the heart grow fonder
Absence makes the bowels yearn stronger
Absence wrings the memory dry—
The pain's enough to make me cry.

Without you here the edges ravel
Without you here my soul won't travel
Without you here I am not free
Without you, dear, I can't find me.

I try to stop the pain I hide
I try to stop the war inside
I try—convince my heart to flee—
My breast laments its casualty.

You come, invade my fortress walls.
You come, I look to you, hope calls.
You come, bearing a humble prize . . .
My heart. Tears cloud my hollow eyes.

My solid mind, it stands aghast
My withered soul reviews the past
My beating heart you hand to me
This truly is too good to be.

I fear to take the eyesore back
My strength resides in what I lack.
I fear you've only come this far
To leave in me the greatest scar.

I hesitate, I pause to stare
I meditate, I see you there.
I palpitate in brief despair
My heart is yours. This is not fair.

I want to have control again
I want you out! But I let you in.
I want to not want you around
But I'm too late; thoughts of you abound.

You offer me a world of peace
You offer me such grand relief
You offer me love, but my trust is dead
The tumult spins inside my head.

I let you in despite my fears
I let you taste my bitter tears
I *let* you. What the hell is that?!
An allowance I cannot retract.

Absence, Oh travesty sublime!
Absence, Hell's intrenchant clime
Absence, the pain I truly fear—
The reason I can't let you near.

I miss you when you're gone away
I miss you at a thought's delay
I miss you when we are not one.
For you, behold, I am undone.

My will conceives its own defense
My will, it pierces all pretense
My will perceives the enemy
But wait, would that be you or me?

I execute the plan prepared
I extricate my heart, ensnared
I execrate what makes me feel
And yet my heart does still appeal.

My hope, it answers my heart's plea
My mind denies its agency
My walls regain its prisoner wise
My true self I compromise.

I fight this losing battle o'er
I fight, your conquest I implore.
I fight, no longer sure just why
I can't give in, but I have to try.

COUNTED FRECKLES

The light, the grandeur, the truth, the worlds
Beyond our sightless eyes
That teem with life, and love, but seem
As counted freckles on nighted skies.

SO MANY REASONS

Your Smile
Because it eases me
Your Hands
Because they wander
Your Heart
Because it sees the good in me
Your Arms
Because I like tattoos (and muscles)
Your Legs
Because they carry around your cute little ass
Your Chest
Because it's my favorite pillow
Your Eyes
Because they speak to me
Your Lips
Because they melt me
Your Nose
Because I love Eskimo kisses
Your Ears
Because they patiently listen to my inane ramblings
Your Laugh
Because it teases and appreciates me
You . . .
Because you're everything I always thought too good to be true.

WHO ARE THE GREAT?

"Who are the great?"
I ask myself, and cannot help but pause
To ponder on the triflings
That lend themselves to obfuscate transcending human cause.

What makes a man?
What represents the sum of who he is?
His thoughts.
What he alone can know—the life only he lives.

A thought—a thing?
A fleeting breath that enters and is gone?
Or does it linger even yet—
A nuance living on?

Perhaps it is the core of being—
This thing, this truth, this thought—
And leaves its trace upon my bones
Rendering a full account, the person I have wrought.

Its origin? Its destiny?
It has no purpose of its own of which I may inquire
But finds its efficacy in yielding
The tenets and the precepts of my heart's every desire.

A blink. A sigh.
A single thought. A curious glistening drop of dew
That rests upon my consciousness
Reflecting and affecting every splinter of my being, everything I say
and do.
It's import? Oh so subtle.
In the aggregate, o'erwhelming.
For the tides, the floods, the waves of thought
They shape the sands—They guide my mind, my heart, my soul
Comprise the furious battle in my head
That in trying to avoid I have only moreso fought.

What denotes man's greatness?
The fruits that burgeon from the flower?
Thoughts are more than thoughts, I think
For they beget, and are from birth, sheathed and filled with power.

FALLEN ANGEL

For all my trying I cannot force
What another does not will.
And yet the strong desire in me,
Despite my valiant efforts to destroy it,
Lives on still.

Once a welcome guest but now
An angel fallen from my grace.
The bittersweet of hope gone sour
I contemplate the devastation,
Salvation absent from this place.

I bring my judgment into question
I can trust myself no more.
For I knew that I was not mistaken
But I was. As I have been before.

SPECULATION

How fickle is the eye
How fickle more the mind.
For the eye's view is but limited
To man and all his kind.

But the mind it knows no limits—
Its endeavors know no bounds
And when it spends its life untrained
It treads on frightful grounds.

BIRTH OF A PROPHET

I see now as I have not before
As the tarrying questions plague me more
The daunting task I ponder o'er
What life does future hold in store?

A veil of calm rests on me now
Bestowed by God someway, somehow
To ease me of my newfound grief,
A false, transient, welcome relief.

I see what I could not for years
I see what I *would* not for years
What I refused with jaded tears
What I drowned out with deafened ears.

But now the prospects of mankind
Grind steadily upon my mind.
No longer leave I the truth behind
Nor fear the truth that I will find.

What felt the prophets of ages lost?
Seeing the whole of time; the cost
To righteousness and civility—
The damage we'd do with our agency.

What were their feelings? What were their cries?
How did they hope in the face of demise?
Wherein lay their faith, their unfaltering path?
How, in the wake of their Sight, did they last?

It's been years from the time I was given a glimpse
And refused it with such tenacious reticence
That for years I've been running, afraid I will see
The truth—that is now clear as day unto me.

The bad I've called "good," and the worse, "not so great"
"Ambitious" for greed, and "frustrated" for hate.
The good, rarely seen, I've mislabeled as "stellar"
Most people, I rationalized, will try to be better.

But time is a teacher, if man will but listen
And deliberate on all things he is given
Clinging to honesty in every instance
Eschewing hypocrisy with fervent resistance.

And what God couldn't give me through vision sublime
Because I refused in my weakness of mind,
He's forbearingly taught me with patience and time
Sparing no smallest effort, my heart to refine.

And now that I'm humbled, sufficiently meek
To give heed to His voice, and believe what He speaks
My heart should burst wide into pieces asunder
My weeping should rival the storm and its thunder

For what I am witness, for what I now see
For the things that are made manifest unto me
For these things that would wring all the life from my soul
And vanquish me in the abyss of their hole—

SHAOLIN POE

And yet God is still merciful, long-suffering, kind
Condescending to nurture my crucified mind
And bestows upon me of His peace and His love
And His message of hope sung from thrones up above.

And veils my rent heart and my world-weary soul
As the truth, to my eyes, he begins to unfold.
That echo of truth that for years left me haunted,
The truth that, before, was much more than I wanted

The truth that did threaten my hope disenchanted
My tradition of faith it, relentless, recanted
The truth that so hindered my indoctrination,
Endangered my pious, confounded "salvation."

But now, in the absence of fear and reproach
Where the kingdom of doubt may no longer encroach
Where tradition is reined and hypocrisy fled
And the whispering lies so explicitly dead,

I am free to see clearly, to ponder, to ask,
Foresee the events that will soon come to pass,
Understand my potential, my calling, my plight,
Discerning mankind in an amplified light.

And I'm bound to exclaim at the things I behold,
For the knowledge that burdens my earth-trodden soul,
For the wisdom e'er wrenching my world-weary soul,
"Woe, woe, woe unto those who are part of the fold."

Thrice woe unto those to whom life has been given
Who are worthy to bow beneath God in His heav'n
Who will live to endure the destruction to come,
The just indignation of Father and Son.

Who will live to endure and to see the world's pains—
The rotting of flesh and decaying remains,
The absence of love, adoration of death
Hell's vengeance for eons of glory bereft.

Hell's vengeance on those who don't choose what is right
Who won't cling to the Lord and abide in His light.
Hell will slaughter, will war, it will hunt, mutilate,
It will plunder, extinguish, and decapitate,

Will yet devastate, ravish, imprison, and torture
Turn father 'gainst son, and mother 'gainst daughter.
And the devil will laugh for the anguish untold
As his bellowing echo will sound 'round the globe.

For this we should fear, for this we should shudder
For this we should strive to unite with each other.
But warnings, supplications, petitions ignored
And records foretelling the punishments stored

Go unnoticed, sit silent, as time subtly races
As man merrily marches his misguided paces
Numb to his coldness that lingers, awaiting
Blind to the sickness, contagious and spreading.

And so we, the righteous, who see what is coming
Who hear Satan's army approaching; their drumming
The drumming of soldiers united in fury,
The drumming of fierceness and anger, so purely

Manifest to our tired, our mendicant souls.
With the drumming, its humming, as ominous tolls—
Steady beat, softly buzzing, its rustling roar
With the quivering, shivering message of war.

19

So thrice woe unto goodness, to kindness, to love
And all that is sanctioned by beings above.
For the foe is decided, alighted, and strong
Determined to turn all that's right into wrong.

But infinite more is the woe unto those
With this knowledge before them, who willingly chose
Of themselves to do wrong and stray from the rod
Then wage battle against their trust brethren in God.

When embattled, distressed, overflowing with grief
It is these who deceivingly offer relief
But then carefully, viciously poison the nectar
Feigning all efforts of offering better.

'Twas of them the Lord spoke when He soberly warned
"For them 'twould be better had they never been born."
Nor exempt are our brethren who chose not to see
As if blindness forgives them their audacity.

For none shall be guiltless where law has been given
And none shall escape the sore judgments of heaven.
Even those who are righteous will barely elude
The destruction to which all the wicked are doomed.

And so I sit quietly, here on my floor
Seeing things with a plainness I hadn't before
A plainness that petrifies me to my core
And I wonder, "What life has the future in store?"

FICTION

Sometimes I dream
When the night is still and the moments flit slowly

Of other wars
Of other gods
Of love and peace and hope and rest

Of other lives
Of other worlds
Of realities I cannot see.

CHROMATIC

Life arrays its colors all
A lovely, rainbow battlefield
The spectrum of emotions flow
To every hue I duly yield.

I get a taste of every hint,
Each tempting tint I come to know
The colors 'compassing me whole
I swim their seas both high and low.

The beauty of the red I see,
Its vein of passion deep and bright.
Has luring lips, exquisite eyes,
And sears the hands that hold too tight.

The yearning and burning, the constantly churning
Of the orangey flames on my sensitive skin.
Flickering, flirting, delightfully dancing—
'Tis a fiery furnace it harbors within.

Grand purple has prospects of power,
Wears regal robes of royalty,
But pomp and pride take precedence—
A vaunted prince—its virtues quickly atrophy.

Grave green with gold and silver gleaming
Catches the eye of every man's heart.
But take care to guard your priorities
For there's little this treasure can't thwart.

Ah, the blue of the peaceful serenity felt
When my soul is assuaged and at rest.
Like the waves of the sea do I lilt upon life,
I feel weighted by no man's behest.

Grim grey is a gutless boring hue
Though inoffensive it may be
Seemingly safe in its simple pursuit,
'Tis the craven that craves mediocrity.

The depths of the black oblivion beckon
Bidding me, begging me come.
Escape, saturation, silence, seclusion,
Solipsism laments its error therefrom.

FORGOTTEN

A moment is an eternity, you know
An infinity within—
As each forever comes and goes
Seizing me with its heaven or hell.

I forget to remember
To step outside, or near to the edge
Of the beads of eternity
Strung together
By the common thread of me.

And I forget to remember
To look beyond myself
To abandon my perspective.
So caught up in nothing—
In vile pearls.

Can I see beyond these bounds?
I press my face to the curved glass
And see my reflection peering back at me.

And I forget to remember
To look beyond myself.
Swimming in infinity

My mind's eye
Pierces the beads of time,
The globes of eternity
And I see through the two-way mirror of sleep.

I have awakened!
I hold eternities in my hand . . .

But I remember to forget.

INTROSPECTION

I see you now as I've been seen
By God above, for years on end
And marvel at the life you lead
Devoid of love, or trust, or friend.

I look at you and see myself
And startle at the things I know
Of where you've been and how you feel
And to what drastic lengths you'll go

To cope; and mold yourself so strict
Adhering to the rules of pain
That dictate what you don't deserve
And what you'll never, ever gain.

I look at you and see myself
And I can scarce hold back my tears
Of watching you do to yourself
What I've done for so many years.

I look at you and my heart weeps
For all the love you haven't known,
For your striking beauty to which you're blind,
For consigning yourself to be alone.

For all the heartache you have borne,
For all the cries no one has heard,
For the dying carefree of your youth
For the mind-rending agony you've endured.

For the soul-killing agony you've endured,
For the heart-wrenching anguish you've embraced
For the sobbing and wailing and beating and tearing,
For every new day you continue to face.

Lost in the motions of habit and proper
Lost in the echoes of tumult and care
Swirling in seas of capsizing emotion
Hopeful and doubtful and loving and scared.

Bearing the burden of those all around you
Weary and withered and worn and afraid;
And shouldering, solo, your cross of conviction,
Constriction, consumption, and forlorn malaise.

I look at you and see myself
With terrifying clarity
With unforgiving soberness
So near to where I used to be.

And yet so far from where I was
As near a shadow follows aft
Lingering a step behind
But merely a form of what has passed.

I LIKE IT HERE

I'm here . . . again.
A popular place to be, really.
Here.
But here hasn't changed so much
Since I was last there.

For the first time in my life
Here is happy, peaceful, still,
Pensive, motivated, encouraged, calm.

I've spent my whole life
Wanting to be there.

Dreaming
Hoping
Wishing
Longing
Yearning

For there.

But for the first time in my life
The First Time
I like it here.

EVOLUTION

I shed the world a piece at a time,
Like an old scaly skin that no longer fits.
As I move and maneuver
I slough off the deadness.

It's hard at times.

A sacrifice, I think.
I'm giving up so much
That's been a part of me for so long.

When I get to higher ground
I look back
And realize the only thing I've shed are fetters.
Beautiful, luring fetters.
Gold chains and decorated bands.

I thought I had treasures
But I only had captivity
Enticing, intriguing, glittering, shiny bondage.
Beautifully wrapped burdens I refused to toss aside
Because of their adornment.

Burdens and fetters I bought and paid for
Expensive, costly encumberment.
I thought I was sacrificing, but I was being freed.

Pieces of world I worked so hard to accumulate
That I coveted.

I am new, evolved, unleashed.

IDIOT QUEEN

"How long has it been?" I ask,
"Some days, a month, a year?"
The pain it flows
It comes and goes
But yet the more the distance grows
The more the pain grows near.

For now that time is not the sole
Thing keeping us apart,
It's safe for me to fell my wall
I slow my pace from run to crawl
And slow it more from crawl to stop
As finally I gather up the pieces of my heart.

I laugh within my sobbing fits
To ridicule myself,
As piece by piece I grieve the mess
My loss of hope and innocence.
For the torn and bloody remnants
I can only blame myself.

Broken? Not the half of it.
Raped—trodden under foot.
Bleeding, weeping, loving still
The one who stole my living will
As if he yet could still fulfill
The chasm in my gut.

"The queen of all that's idiot!"
My solvent shout resounds
I should know much better at my age
My honed discernment sure can gauge
The false and hypocritical face
That in this world abounds.

But as I pause to let me grieve
A voice within my head
Rebukes me for my narrow sight
For loving what is far from right
And bids me leave it and press on.
Let the dead bury their dead.

INARTICULATE

Words would be a poor man's choice to tell you how I feel.

Words fail me, my love.
This deepening river of emotion coursing through my veins
Overflows its bounds and renders me speechless.

I try...
But the words fail me, my love.

So I look to others to find my verse
And while I know they've felt the same
Their words, as well, do blush with shame

To elucidate, yes, to clearly convey
The evolution transforming me each passing day
Ever mounting and shifting in lurid array
With a rapidity subduing my need to assay--

To scrutinize; Speeding the essence of time
With no language to speak—nor declaration sublime
Enough to express the new me that is mine
Or to key in the heart to the cues of my rhyme.

I yearn to reveal, I pine to impart,
I tremble to whisper the truth of my heart
But taut tangles of thought knot my well-groomed remarks--
I'm inclined to abandon this path I've embarked.

Yet I must make a record of the me that I was
And accordingly annotate the source of the cause
That moved heav'n and earth to create, unrenowned
The me that I am...the once lost, but now found.

I'm a fountain of hope—reborn, to be true
For the love and the hope and the life that is you.

You, and you only, unpolluted my heart.
You, and you only, dared I trust from the start.
With a patience supreme you undevastated my soul.
With a tenderness unmatched you again made me whole.

The life-long loss of fear and woe you've accomplished within me
A Herculean feat at least, impossible at best
And when you've given me all that you are
You give me of your rest.

I have no gift to give you back
No means to pay this glorious debt.
It is because of you and you only
That I'm able to move forward without fear of regret.

I must here pause to criticize
The shallowness of my conveyance.
Am I so bankrupt of expression?
Am I a desert? A drought of song?

As I try to place my heart on paper
My feelings are like a budding rose,
But as words, they wither—a fleeting vapor
In the languishing wake of inarticulate repose.

So thus I paint my thoughts askance
In a pallid and two dimensional stance
With the hope that perspective and time perchance
May render a hue of intention.

But suffice it to say in this time in this place
I want to study your soul and every inch of your face
'Til I know every nuance and flavor of grace...

You are my kingly, my steadfast, my modest-bedecked lover
...my gift from God.

DISSOLUTION

I've died as to my strength of will
The ruse my dreams built on is killed.
The future I envisioned—dead.
No trust remains to take its stead.

My hope is wrung dry, my face sodden with tears,
My heart stripped of the treasure it clung to for years.

I'm alone in a world full of clamoring action.

BE HAPPY

At last my mind is still again
And so, in keeping, stills my pen
I know not to whom this message goes forth
Whether foe, or stranger, or friend.

Just be mindful in reading
Of the drum you are beating
That keeps you in time with what tune

For the beat that is calling,
The song that is playing,
Should be meant for your pleasure and boon.

YOU

Despite the paths I choose to take,
No matter what I say or do,
My heart relentlessly reminds
And always brings me back to you.

Your essence dances in my mind
Though someone I have never met.
And though I try unceasingly
I'm never able to forget . . . you.

But yet to say I always try
Would not entirely be true.
Sometimes I sit and watch you dance—
My hopes have grown quite fond of you.

And yet I fear the punishment
Of loving you so pure and deep.
For nothing but the sorest pain
Can come from what I cannot keep . . . that's you.

For I feel within my hope of hopes
In the innermost longing of my heart
That our time together will be too brief
And then forever I'll be apart . . . from you.

WHAT IS REAL?

The past is mostly lost to me,
Faded memories what I see,
Examining reality
I wonder how much I perceive
When all I have of what I've lived is nothing but a memory.

The bits I salvage of my past,
Clips of pictures that will not last.
Nostalgic feelings fading fast
As time evaporates millions of moments
My head is hung, my mind aghast.

For what cause do I live each day
When every detail fades away?
I hope for things that cannot stay.
A moment lives and then is dead.
The tiny life span I replay.

Memories are not what is real
So why can they change what I feel?
The whole of reality is so surreal,
A grand façade that I live out,
An aching wound that will not heal.

SHAOLIN POE

So why not live my life in dreams?
For nothing can be what it seems.
Behind true objects moonlight beams
Casting shadows on the floor.
Reality and reverie intertwining at the seams.

The shadows dance upon the floor
Their laughter rolls, their voices roar
Indicative of something more
Reality must be close, nearby
I search blindly, bloody fingers, looking for the door.

Wherein is reality?
Within the hopes of futurity?
Within the realm of history?
A hope is a dream, until a memory it becomes.
Can reality transcend me?

Or is it limited to my narrow scope
And the impenetrable walls at which I grope?
The thoughts within my head elope
Reality is lost to me
That it exists outside of me is all that I can hope.

IF NOTHING ELSE

If nothing else remember this
You cannot stop the fight inside
You cannot yield to others' whims
You must be true to who you are
Or self-destruct in your effort to conform.

There is no happiness to be had in the pleasing of another
True joy comes from peace with one's self.

MERCURIAL

Hope can be capricious
When least your mind is set
Upon the things you love and dream.
When it wanders into how things seem
And takes you on a journey
From blissful joy to sore regret.

So be prudent in your thoughts
But more so in your doubts
Never fear to chase your dreams,
Disregarding how things seem
Focusing on things you want,
Not your current whereabouts.

GIVE ME A MOMENT

Give me yet a moment
To cling to that which I
Was raised to trust and hope and love
Before I let it die.

A wilderness of apathy
Is the future I now see.
I cannot dream a thought or scene,
My joy is lost to me.

My thoughts, they wander listlessly
Bereft of all but grief
Distress for what I must discard—
The whole of my belief.

Belief in lies, in fairy tales
Wrapped rich in ornament
For which I bought and begged and burned—
My daily sacrament.

A sacrament of lies and gall,
A sacrament indeed,
Sweet poison to the mind and soul,
Sweet drug that I now need.

I know it sows the death of me
But stronger do I crave
My drug, to soothe these seeping wounds—
My master, and my slave.

I cannot quick let go of that
Which was for all my life
My hope, my dream, my secret strength,
My sole retreat in strife.

And so I mourn and fight and gnash
And bitterly I cry.
But I cannot forsake the truth
For the comfort of a lie.

And so I humbly beg of you . . . to

Give me yet a moment
To cling to that which I
Was raised to trust and hope and love
Before I let it die.

FORBEARANCE

The secretest wishes of my heart
You've given them to me.
The life I tried to live—a lie—
Lies deadened at my feet.

I knew I couldn't trust, I knew!
I knew I'd never love.
But by God's grace I chanced on you,
A seraph from above.

You found me locked away
High up
Within my tower secure.

But
slowly,
carefully,
patiently,

You disengaged
the locks,
the bolts,
the safety nets,
the barbs of hate.

SHAOLIN POE

My weapons of distrust you crushed.

And
fearlessly,
magnificently,
You fended off
The who that I was not.

Defenseless, timid, I stood alone
My rawest self, encased in stone
And through the stalwart door you walked
Understanding of my pain.

'Twas not to rescue that you came
'Twas not to claim or ransom gain
'Twas merely to love, and not in vain
That you entered my sanctum of hurt.

In your eyes I saw knowledge of grief I had borne,
Of my once vibrant spirit, now dim and forlorn.
You possessed wisdom, insight, and burden long borne
And a fading, receding anticipation of love.

You showed me your anguish, you showed me your heart
And you didn't intrude—you did only impart.
You appeared so sincere, so steadfast, so smart,
Regarding the matters that weighed on my soul.

You stood very still, in no hurry to go
And I wanted you to stay; I craved for you to stay.
For you were like no one I'd ever known
But I dared not admit my desire, my vulnerability, my utter weakness.

You bid me to speak, but I held my tongue
So you spoke to me softly and enjoyed my silence.
You did nothing to force and would have left at my wish
Thus you won my undying alliance.

For in all of the years in my tower so high
With its locks and its barriers reaching the sky
With my heart turned to stone and my tears long since dry
I'd forgotten the hope of my heart.

But you reminded me . . .
And I knew, in that moment, I loved you.

BE STILL

Silence.
Peace.
Serenity.
Transient moments routinely forgot.
But when tranquility tiptoes into my being
My thoughts with frantic are fraught.

Calm.
Stillness.
Quiescence.
All states of being for which I should pine.
And yet when they stumble upon me by chance
I endeavor to hasten the time.

Noise.
Commotion.
Hullaballoo.
A world where convenience is king.
Unceasingly arduous, wearing, and aging
But regardless I steadfastly cling.

Be at peace with myself?
I can't calm the mayhem in my soul.
Forsake the impious and desire the pure?
Lost in business, I am far from whole.

VOCIFEROUS

I want to write, I want to write!
It bids me burn my midnight oil
When obligations beg for sleep
So I can run man's race once more.

My heart is changed,
My song is begun
I can never go back to my view of before

I hear the call
And it beckons me forth
And I must answer forevermore.

ZEALOT

Glory? To ascend to Thee
The Most High and only true God.
The means by which I attain such a prize?
Holding on to the iron rod.

The mists of darkness which lurk all about?
An attempt to distract me from my goal.
The fruit of the tree that is whiter than white?
The blessing for those who are part of the fold.

So what of all else that pertains not to such
Glory and motion and tension and strife?
Is not all part of one and one part of all
Pertaining to either damnation or life?

Then all is of import and all is of cause,
And purpose and meaning and sway
To keep us from error or lead us thereto
As we walk on or stray from the chosen way.

Then arises the question that plays on, that plagues,
That distresses my circumscribed mind:
How is this path of righteousness to my senses, my conscious
My heart, and my soul, to the core of my being defined?

How with a body of matter that's gross
And corporeal senses and stays
Can I discern an eternity—or segment thereof—
It's spiritual light and its rays?

For inspiration is quiet, is peaceful, serene,
And discord and tumult flood the ears of my soul.
Confusion abounds and evil pervades,
Seductively decaying what used to be whole.

I strain to make sense and warn those I know
Of the subtle ways that they might be deceived
But not only do dear friends become deaf to truth
But turn from what they used to believe.

The voice of my Master is strong yet genteel
And I struggle to hear it and know
With a surety that what I embrace as a truth
Is sent from above and not the result of deception below.

So to whom do I look? To my God.
For there is none other constant of which I'm aware.
My trust is implicit, my faith truly blind,
My hope in Him only for none other can bear

Or can carry the weight of my hopes, and my dreams,
And my trust, and my love, and my sin.
And none other can comfort, console, or can succor,
As He whom the grave did not win.

On what sense, then, do I rely for truth
That I may be sure not to falter or fall?
I rely on that Holy Spirit of Promise
The gift I am given that is greater than all.

The large and spacious building is grand and is dark
And many there be that enter in at that gate
But to me it is given to love and to serve
And to save all I can before it's too late.

For today is the day to perform my labors,
For the time when night cometh is nigh.
And then it's too late, for no sorrow for sin
Nor labor can undo that eternal tie.

They are they who are bound and are chained
By the bands of death and of hell
And regret for eternity their awful misdeeds
And their suffering no man can tell.

But for those who partook of the fruit of the tree
Of light, and of love, and of life
And were not dissuaded from their righteous path
By persecution from those in the building of strife

Have nothing to fear for they truly are saved—
Have endured the test and proved themselves true
Have held steadfast, giving no credence to numbers
For those who enter in at the strait gate are few.

But for those who partook of the love of God
And then were ashamed and turned 'round,
'Tis a bitter consequence they must face
For no place in heaven for them shall be found.

Worlds without end are saved for the true,
The disciples, the brethren of Christ
Who gave all of themselves, all they had in this world—
Who sacrificed,

Endured 'til their lives were all spent.
"And this is eternal life that they may know thee the only true God
and Jesus Christ whom thou hast sent."

AN ODE TO LIFE

Don't mock me life
For I have no patience today.

My fun is gone
I am worry-worn
And I can't come out to play.

But perchance on the morrow
When we meet again
I will have some hope to spare...

And if I do
Come find me quick
And mock
And we can share.

For another laugh
Is what I crave
And all my joy is there.

POST A REVIEW

Thanks so much for reading my collection of poetry! I'd appreciate it tremendously if you took a moment to review my book. These poems were written over a couple of decades. As my first published work, it took a lot of time and effort to put together and publish. It was truly a labor of love.

My goal with this book is to touch the hearts and minds of those who read it—to let people know they are not alone in their doubt, their love, their pain, and their wanderings. I want to remind people that when we feel most alone, we are having a common human experience that has been shared by millions around the world.

Reviews help greatly toward that end. I read every review I get, and take the feedback to heart. I look forward to hearing what you think!

ACKNOWLEDGMENTS

I have to start my thanking my amazing husband. I've tried a lot of different endeavors and hobbies over the years, and he never tells me I'm crazy or wasting my time. He supports me and does whatever he can to help me be successful. My love, thank you so much. I wouldn't be where I am in life without you.

I also have to thank my dear friend Sara. I think of her as my partner in literary crime. She has been an incredible cheerleader throughout this process. She read my drafts and gave me her thoughts on many aspects of this undertaking. Her enthusiasm kept me going.

Last but not least, I need to give a shout out to my book club. They were tremendously supportive of my efforts and gave me feedback whenever I asked for it. You ladies are awesome!

ABOUT THE AUTHOR

Shaolin Poe is the pen name for a husband and wife writing duo. Shaolin is a combination of their first names, and Poe is an homage to Edgar Allen Poe. They met in the military while flying on the same spy plane. They love to transport readers to unexpected places and showcase the humor of situations. When they aren't writing, they enjoy music, traveling, board games, and stand-up comedy.

Additional note: While this book was written exclusively by the female half of the writing team, she couldn't have done it without the help of her husband. This book of poetry is also quite different from the novels they write, but it was important to her to publish it because she has a profound love for poetry.

Made in United States
North Haven, CT
27 April 2023

35965377R00036